C000221149

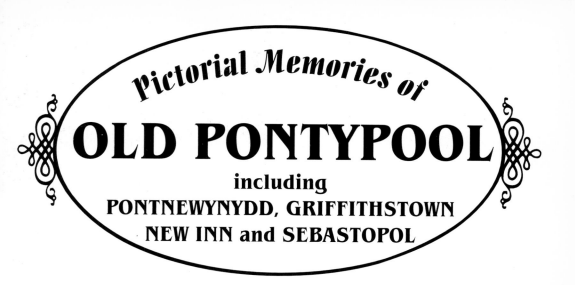

Pictorial Memories of
OLD PONTYPOOL
including
PONTNEWYNYDD, GRIFFITHSTOWN
NEW INN and SEBASTOPOL

by Bryan Roden

Foreword by
Peter Phillips
Headmaster West Monmouth School

Volume 1

Old Bakehouse Publications

Abertillery

© Bryan Roden

First published in September 1998
Reprinted in February 1999

All rights reserved

The right of Bryan Roden to be identified
as author of this work has been asserted in
accordance with sections 77 and 78 of the
Copyright Designs and Patents Act 1988.

ISBN 1 874538 86 7

Published in the U.K. by
Old Bakehouse Publications
Church Street,
Abertillery, Gwent NP3 lEA
Telephone: 01495 212600 Fax: 01495 216222

Made and printed in the UK
by J.R. Davies (Printers) Ltd.

This book is sold subject to the condition that it shall not,
by way of trade or otherwise be lent, resold, hired out,
or otherwise circulated without the publisher's prior consent
in any form of binding or cover other than that in which it is
published and without a similar condition, including this
condition, being imposed upon the subsequent purchaser.
No part of this publication may be reproduced, stored in a retrieval
system, or transmitted in any form or by any means electronic,
mechanical, photographic, recording or otherwise, without
prior permission of the author and/or publishers.

Foreword

by Peter Phillips, M.Sc, M.Ed, C. Math, FIMA, FRGS, FRSA.
Headmaster West Monmouth School

"Someone said that God gave us memory so that we might have roses in December"
J.M. Barrie (1860-1937)

I believe this is a very appropriate moment for the Headmaster of West Monmouth School to write the foreword to a book on Old Pontypool.

It was in 1898 the first pupil was admitted to Jones' West Monmouth School and as 'Pictorial Memories of Old Pontypool' is published, the school has reviewed, quite properly, its own history and success and, in so doing has been reminded of the strong umbilical cord which links it to Pontypool and the surrounding communities. All at West Mon have been reminded, if reminding is necessary, how proud we are, and have been, to be part of the history of Pontypool.

For my small part, I have been Headmaster at West Monmouth School since 1988 and I have been invited to write this foreword: for both opportunities, I am privileged.

In this excellent book, Bryan Roden has weaved a historical perspective of Pontypool, including Pontnewynydd, New Inn, Griffithstown and Sebastopol, that stretches back 120 years. Cleverly, it takes the reader on a journey from the Town Centre to all the surrounding satellite communities: pleasingly, for an educationalist, it devotes a whole chapter to 'Schooldays'. From the 'best days of your life', it explores local religion, historic buildings, sport, entertainment, trading, industry and the railway. It concludes with a series of fascinating 'then and now' photographs.

Most readers, like me, will discover quickly that very many of the photographs are 'new' to them: few, in fact, having been previously published. All readers, including myself, will be grateful that Bryan Roden has researched this presentation so thoroughly and arranged it so logically.

'Pictorial Memories of Old Pontypool' is an easy 'to read' book but allow yourself lots of time: the photographs on every page will entice many memories, or speculations, which will make the reader's progress pleasingly slow, particularly so, if you choose to share your journey simultaneously with others: well done Bryan Roden!

fugit irreparabile tempus (we cannot stop time in its tracks).

Peter Phillips

Contents

Introduction

The written history of Pontypool and the surrounding area can be traced back a number of centuries. Unfortunately the camera did not arrive until the nineteenth century and accordingly, good quality pictorial records of early life are in limited supply. However, for some years I have been an enthusiastic collector of picture postcards and illustrated material connected with the district.

To this end therefore, and as we approach the close of the twentieth century, I felt it appropriate to produce a visual record of the past 120 years through the medium of this book. The photographs included are virtually all previously unpublished and I hope that everyone will enjoy them to the full.

I have tried to make the range of topics covered as comprehensive as possible, the underlying theme however is one of photographic memories to remind us of a distinguished past. The opening chapter deals with Pontypool Town Centre, much of which may be difficult to recognise by today's standards. The views of old George Street are perfect examples of this situation.

There is mention of some 'good old-fashioned' traders of the town, such as Fowler's, Sandbrook and Dawe and Daniel's the grocers - all three being long gone, but not forgotten by many. Most of the outlying areas are also acknowledged, as Pontypool's boundaries stretch afar; 100-year old pictures of Griffithstown and New Inn have been included to confirm this. Later chapters provide the necessary reminders that Pontypool once had half a dozen railway stations within its borders until the 1960s. That total has now been reduced to just one at Pontypool Road, New Inn.

Time was, when forges, collieries, steelmaking and the spinning of man-made fibres provided the essential employment for the population. The last 25 years have changed all that; the prime example being the once vast British Nylon Spinner's workforce, these days reduced to just two or three per-cent of its peak totals.

Religious establishments too have suffered somewhat in this changing world, with a number of one-time welcoming churches and chapels locking their doors for the last time. Thankfully however, all is not lost in melancholy amongst our places of heritage. The preservation of such landmarks as The Folly and The Grotto, inspired by groups of devoted promoters is to be saluted.

The educational interests are catered for, with amongst others, the earliest known photograph of West Mon School, seen during its construction in the year 1897. To publish a book about the district of Pontypool without mention of its sports men and women would be unforgivable, there are therefore a few memorable pictures included to cater for such interests.

Finally, there is a chapter devoted to a collection of local scenes as they appeared many years ago and which have been re-photographed from the very same spot in 1998. This chapter above all will probably do most to illustrate the enormity of how things have changed in the district, for better or worse, these past one hundred years.

Bryan Roden

CHAPTER 1
Pontypool Town Centre

1. What at one time might have been described as 'The Gateway To Pontypool', is this spot at Hanbury Road looking towards the Town Hall. This particular photograph shows a quiet scene from about 1914 with Mount Pleasant Church on the left. Along the right-hand side can be seen an extended stone-built wall which has long since been removed, the area now being a stopping point for public transport.

2. An early morning scene with the Town Hall clock showing five minutes to nine. The period is about 1905 and pre-dates the building of the library. The road surface is still a little primitive, it not receiving an updated hard asphalt finish until the early 1920s, following the introduction of a regular public transport service to the town.

3. Looking from Commercial Street towards Hanbury Road and the period has advanced to the year 1960. There are a few former landmarks to remember such as the Abersychan and Pontypool Co-op Store, W.H. Smith for stationery and Briggs Ltd. selling footwear and clothing. On the extreme right is Glantorfaen House (The Municipal Buildings).

4. Looking up a busy Commercial Street some 80 years ago. Careful study of this photograph reveals 'A sale of stock' at Woolley's Stores which is attracting a crowd of onlookers, whilst some period delivery carts also block the road. Immediately on the right of the picture is The Park Temperance Hotel and Restaurant, with Mr. Sansome's Dental Surgery close by.

5. The years continue to move on in Commercial Street, the period now being the early 1930s. The days of prolonged traffic congestion have yet to come and shoppers can walk freely along the road. The first shop to be seen on the right belonged to The Abersychan Co-operative Society, which in the previous photograph was the premises of The Park Temperance Hotel and Restaurant. These days it is occupied by Pontypool Community Council.

6. This view from the late 1940s is bound to revive a few memories concerning the number of busy shops that once adorned 'this part of town'. The lone car is parked outside Cash Hardware Stores, whilst next door is C.H. Pearce the furnishers who opened for business in the town in 1920. Next door again is the ever popular Longstaff's Bazaar. On the opposite side of the street is another collection of well-established businesses such as Fulgoni's Cafe, Dewhurst the butchers and W. Morgan James, the chemist and optician.

7. Here is an opportunity to look in the opposite direction and be reminded yet again of the changing face of Commercial Street. The George Hotel is prominent on the right with the former London Hosiery shop on the opposite corner. At the time of publication of this book, this one-time fashion store has become a Video shop. Further along the street on the left-hand side it will be noticed that the Pearl Assurance House has yet to be built.

8. Looking up Crane Street from The Cross in the year 1905 and there is much to see. Immediately on the right-hand corner was a favourite grocery shop 'Peglers', a business that was originally started in Pontypool in 1847. Close-by can be seen the sign of leading ironmongers of the town, Sandbrook and Dawe's. This concern was founded even earlier, in 1817 by one Charles Davies, eventually closing in 1989, and thereby signalling the end of an era. On the other side of the street is the old White Lion public house and this building, after closure as licensed premises, was incorporated into the large shop of E. Fowler and Son.

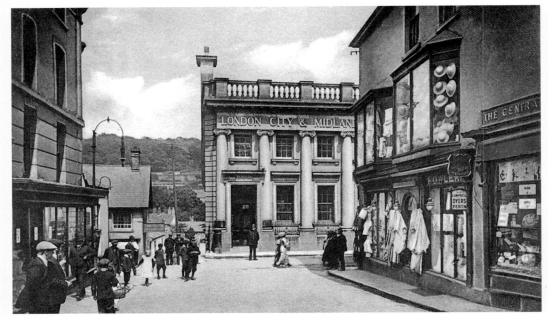

9. The Cross, a latter-day name for the junction between George Street, Commercial Street and Crane Street. This is a typical Edwardian scene from 1910 and the local 'Bobby' is on duty outside what is now the Midland Bank. On the right, Fowler's have an exterior display of goods for sale.

10. Crane Street is yet another part of Pontypool that has changed considerably, much of it beyond recognition in recent times. Somewhat adorned with places of liquid refreshment, a few of those places can be seen in this early photograph. On the left are The Three Cranes and The Swan, with The Globe just opposite. Further down the street is the one-time popular outfitting and clothing shop of D.W. Simpson, perhaps better remembered in later years as Hodges Ltd.

11. A little further down Crane Street at the beginning of the twentieth century. To be seen is the butcher's shop of The English and Colonial Meat Company which was next door to the original building of The Ship Hotel; the hotel being extensively altered a few years after this picture was taken. Adjoining The Ship was Walkers Waverley Hotel, an establishment which catered for the more temperate members of the community at the time.

12. In this early scene from about 1903, a crew of window cleaners busy themselves at the London and Provincial Bank (now Barclays). A gentleman stands outside The George Hotel, which is seen with its earlier frontage before major alterations took place in 1905. The front part of the hotel was at one time a watchmaker and jeweller's shop.

13. Market Street in about 1905 with the town's market on the left, a building which has stood the test of time for more than a hundred years. Taking some eighteen months to build, this prestigious market place was opened amid much local celebration in December 1894. A few more old establishments on the right are, The Market Tavern, Paulett the fruit and fish merchant and yet another public house, The Winning Horse.

14. Old George Street besieged with pedestrians rather than traffic in this picture from about 1908. Always the town's 'bottleneck', great play was made in the year 1899 with the road being widened from 14 feet to 20 feet; this was seen as the final solution to the town centre's continued congestion. On the right hand corner is The Old Bath Beer House, possibly the earliest inn in the town, it eventually being pulled down in 1951. Finally on July 10th 1963, the great demolition of this side of George Street began, with the clearance of many buildings as far as the Post Office, thus changing the face forever.

15. A closer look at the London and Provincial Bank and the flamboyant buildings belonging to Fowlers Lion House. The Greyhound Hotel is seen with some ornate lighting and next to the market entrance is the bootmaker's shop of Frank Parkhouse.

16. George Street as it appeared in the early 1900s. On the extreme right is The Castle Hotel, when Mr. James Gunn was the proprietor and next door was to be found a fashionable business of years gone by, that of a 'Pawnbroker'. The tall pine-ended building, a little further down the street was The Crown Hotel. This venue was the turning point for horse-drawn brakes during their journeys between Abersychan and Pontypool. The next official stop would be the Theatre Royal in Osborne Road to collect passengers for their return trip.

17. A far more modern look at George Street, this time during the 1950s. Some more busy shops to note are Stead and Simpson for footwear and of course F.W. Woolworth who first came to Pontypool in 1923 and are still there to this day. Past 'regulars' will remember The Full Moon public house, from where this photograph was taken, and later to be demolished during the widening of George Street. The licence of this pub was transferred to new premises, The New Moon at Trevethin in 1965.

18. A most impressive view of George Street in 1930s style. There are some familiar shop signs hanging above, such as Liptons the grocers, Deans the outfitters and Boots the chemists.

19. Upper Park Terrace, an area which began to develop with the opening of the railway link with Newport in 1852. This event soon brought increased trade and prosperity to the town, with the new station at Crane Street opening in 1858. The building of Park Terrace was completed by 1859 and had a commanding view over the station. On this photograph a young lad is seen with his delivery cart from Cummings Boot Repairers of No.37 Crane Street.

CROSS BOOT WAREHOUSE,

3, Commercial Street, PONTYPOOL,

191

Branch:
Cash Boot Stores,
2, Commercial Street,
PONTNEWYDD.

Dr. to R. WILLIAMS,

WHOLESALE AND RETAIL

BOOT & SHOE MANUFACTURER.

Terms Cash . . .

Repairs by . . .
Experienced . . .
Workmen . . .

Every description of
Boots & Shoes
made to order . .

The sizes & fittings .
of all goods sold are .
registered for . . .
further reference . .

George Street, Feby 20 1907
PONTYPOOL,

Miss Truman

Bought of

Charles & Sons

Boot & Shoe Manufacturers.

20. Some early advertising from two local boot and shoe manufacturers. These were the golden years when customers could choose their particular design of footwear and watch it being made to order on the premises.

21. A tranquil Osborne Road in 1903. On the right is the once-spacious General Post Office which also housed Pontypool's telephone exchange and its host of telephonists, before the arrival of modern automatic systems in the late 1960s. Next door is an Army Recruitment Office, and the most prominent building on the opposite side of the road is that popular landmark, The Theatre Royal. Built in the late nineteenth century, it served as a public assembly hall, a variety theatre and eventually, to be probably better remembered, one of Pontypool's cinemas. The Royal finally closed its doors in 1958, the first victim of the run of closures of the town's picture houses.

22. Another peaceful view of Osborne Road, this time looking south. Originally known as Manchester Road, it was later re-named Osborne after the nearby Osborne Forge. There will be few readers who will not recognise the building on the left as The Griffin Press, one of Pontypool's longest established companies. The building has however now been converted into a number of flats.

23. A scene from the year 1900 showing part of the old Town Bridge before the complete re-building of 1924. Immediately left is the present-day Rugby Club adjacent to T.A. Jones the photographers. The building on the right is the Old Bell Inn, later to be converted into Park Cottages which are currently in a state of abandonment.

24. A pre-war scene at Clarence Corner, the once popular stopping place for the valley's bus services. One of the forerunners to provide a regular passenger service was The Eastern Valley Motor Services Ltd., a company formed in 1921 by the Barrett family. In turn, this company was taken over in about 1928 by what was to become a household name for bus travellers, 'The Western Welsh'. Behind the bus on the right is The Clarence Hotel, and it is seen in days of a certain affluence; now after 200 years of firm standing it has unfortunately become a sad sight in Pontypool.

25. Clarence Corner, quite a number of years later during the 1960s. The area is still seen as a centre of bus-route activity, although increased volumes of traffic have necessitated the enlarged facilities. The '1960s' was the period of the withdrawal of rail passenger services in the eastern and western valleys. With private motoring yet to take hold, these were halcyon days for the local bus companies. In the background of this photograph can be seen the offices of the Red and White Company and that memorable refreshment haunt, The Carlton Cafe.

CHAPTER 2

Out of Town

26. The Post Office and General Stores in Rockhill Road Pontymoyle (note the alternative spelling) in 1915. Miss Doris Magall is stood at the gate and at this time the premises also served as a cabinet maker's, upholsterer, French polisher and house furnisher's. This branch Post Office closed for business in the 1990s.

27. Great Western House, which was one of twelve houses called Great Western Terrace at Pontymoile. Built in about 1866 to house members of the locomotive staff at Pontypool Road, the terrace was demolished in 1980 with the exception of Great Western House itself. It being the most opulent house in the row, it was originally built for a senior railway company employee and the building still survives to this day as 'Fountain House'.

28. This original picture postcard is captioned 'A Bird's Eye View of Pontymoile' and dates from about 1930. Looking carefully, one can identify a few landmarks of yesteryear, such as the chimney stack of the Pontypool Foundry and Engineering Company in the right foreground. To the right of centre is Cwmynyscoy viaduct with Pontymoile Mission Hall in the centre.

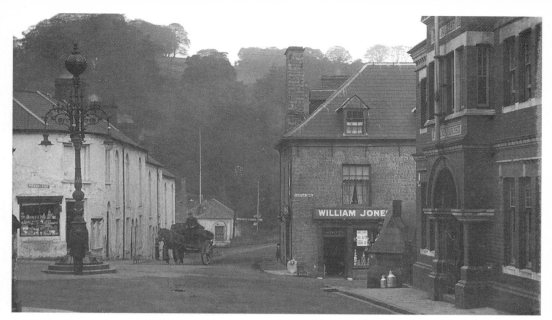

29. Pontymoile Corner viewed from just below the old railway bridge in 1914. On the right are the offices of the old Panteg Urban District Council and the elegant water fountain. This fountain was placed in memory of Catherine Williams, wife of long-serving Council Chairman, Alfred Williams. It was to Alfred Williams that the most ornate lamp was dedicated, as seen on the left of the picture. The lamp has been preserved and re-located behind the buildings to the right. In the background is a corner grocery shop, owned at the time by Mr William Jones. Originally this building housed one of the infamous 19th Century 'Truck Shops'.

30. This picture was taken just a few metres away from the previous photograph and signals the beginning of the end for old Pontymoile. Demolition of the railway bridge is taking place following the closure of the line from Pontypool Road Station, the area having been a motorists' nightmare with everlasting traffic hold-ups. Also seen here is the old Mission Hall, since demolished and replaced by a new building in Rockhill Road.

31. A scene looking from a position just behind the now disappeared Clarence Street Station, the platform of which displays a few familiar advertisements. This general view shows Mill Road Trosnant, the gasworks, the disused malthouse, Woolley's Garage and The Clarence Hotel. The majority of these buildings have now disappeared, one of the exceptions being a rapidly deteriorating hotel.

32. The former Eastern Valley railway line pictured just between Blaendare Road Halt and Cwmynyscoy Viaduct, showing a goods train with a banker engine travelling down the valley. To the left can be seen a group of houses known as 'Daisy View', with some land on the right of the railway line being utilised as a vegetable plot.

33. Victoria Road Blaendare on a quiet day some years past. The girls' pinafore dresses and a rudimentary road surface suggest the period to be about 1905. Any visitor returning to the Blaendare area will probably be quite astonished at the transformation caused by the long-thought-necessary by-pass system.

34. Looking up Blaendare Road some 75 years ago with its late Edwardian-style houses on the left-hand side of the hill. On the opposite side was the lodge and drive leading to West Mon School. At the bottom of the road, residents will remember the narrow bridge that once passed over the railway and Blaendare Halt.

35. Penygraig Terrace, which may well have acquired its name in the same manner as nearby Rockhill Road. During excavation in 1981, road builders working in the area found a solid wall of rock formation and of course, from the Welsh language, 'Pen' means 'Top' and 'Craig' means 'Rock'. At the end of the street is a 'HFB' delivery horse and cart; this would have belonged to Hanbury Farmhouse Bread, their bakery being situated at Pontymoile.

36. The splendidly-built houses of Park View which were mostly completed by the early 1900s, shortly before this particular photograph was taken. Once overlooking the main Pontypool Road to Crumlin railway line, the scene today is of a newly constructed roadway.

37. Albion Road, facing in a westerly direction, an early highway of Pontypool. It was built by the Abercarn Highway Trustees and opened in the year 1820 to provide access to the Old Furnace. Two neighbouring public houses are seen on the left-hand side of the road, The Unicorn and The Albion Inn of which only The Unicorn building still stands.

38. Albion Road again, this time looking eastwards and the period is similar to the previous view, about 1906. Albion Road was the main road from Pontypool to the western valleys before the new road as we know it today was opened in 1988. To assist today's reader, the gas standard on the right of the road approximately marks the spot where the junction now leads to the new Crumlin Road.

39. An exceptional photograph looking down Trosnant Street, one of the oldest and once most populated districts of Pontypool. Around the time of this photograph, the following interesting report was made by the County Medical Officer to the Sanitary Committee on 14th January 1910.

"Trosnant - This is the oldest portion of the Urban District and in it we found dwelling houses varying very much in degree of fitness for habitation. Nos. 21-28 form a group which call for definite sanitary improvements. Some have no through ventilation, others are damp and defective, whilst a few have filthy bedding with vermin-infested bedrooms. Nos. 30 and 32 - The WC consists of a hand-flushed hopper situated on the side of, and slightly to the rear of the kitchen. These should be superseded by a flush tank. For in the case of No. 32 the hopper was in a deplorably filthy and offensive condition."

40. A 1930s view showing Cwmynyscoy Viaduct. This viaduct was built by contractor Stephen Thomas for the Monmouthshire Railway and Canal Company. This important structure was opened on June 30th 1852, and has only been demolished in recent years as part of the new road scheme. The houses on the left are 'School View' which overlooked the former Pontymoile School.

41. The 'long-lost' Glyn Pond in the Crumlin Valley (Cwm Glyn Valley). The ponds were originally constructed during the 18th Century as intended water feeders to the Town Forge and Glyn Furnace. Water from here was also channelled to the Monmouthshire Canal which ran from Pontnewynydd to Newport. Also to be seen is the boatman's cottage on the left and the former railway route to Hafodyrynys and Crumlin, along the water's edge.

42. Wainfelin Road with its busy corner Post Office, Newsagent's and Confectioner's. The year is 1910 and the Sub-Postmaster in Wainfelin at the time was Mr. William Thomas. Nowadays this shop forms two separate entities, a fish and chip shop and an off-licence.

43. This time the cameraman has moved a little further along Wainfelin Road. The gentleman on the right is stood at the junction with Wainfelin Avenue and, just beyond can be seen the old George Street School. This school had 140 years of teaching to its credit before eventual demolition in 1989.

44. The photographic tour of old Wainfelin continues in Fowler Street some 90 years ago. The scene shows fashionable Edwardian style housing, with the road surface and pedestrian pavements awaiting further improvement. In the distance an old-fashioned steam roller is just emerging around the corner, busy doing its duty.

45. A view of Bushy Park which also shows a building of some historical interest in the centre of the picture. This building dates from around 1690 and has a number of uses to its credit. In the twentieth century it has been a pig farm, then Nos. 4 and 5 Penywain Cottages, finally being converted into a single dwelling in the 1960s. Complete renovation has now transformed this 300 year-old structure. The other cottages on the right were demolished to make way for Llanerch Close and the land in the foreground is now the home of Pontypool United R.F.C.

PEAKE'S
BUS & COACH PROPRIETORS
Funeral Furnishers, Undertakers

CREMATIONS ARRANGED
Rolls-Royce Hearse and Cars
SALOON & ALL-WEATHER COACHES
WEDDINGS, CONCERTS &
OUTING PARTIES CATERED FOR
QUOTATIONS FREE

**WESLEY GARAGE, HANBURY RD.
PONTNEWYNYDD, MON.**
Telephone : PONTYPOOL 44

PHONE 229 PONTYPOOL

RADIO
ELECTRICAL
TELEVISION

With the Very Best
"After Sales Service"

CHALONER BROS.
(PONTYPOOL) LTD.

PONTNEWYNYDD

George Farr
PAWNBROKER,   ETC.
3 Market Street, Pontypool

MONEY LENT ON MOST KINDS OF PORTABLE GOODS.   LOW CHARGES
Unredeemed Pledges always on sale.

46. It is some years since Pontnewynydd looked like this. In the distance on the hillside is the now-closed hospital and a little nearer to the eye is The Horseshoe Hotel. The railway station is on the left of this picture and in close proximity, are some industrial buildings which probably form part of the old Pontnewynydd Galvanising Works.

47. From the year 1905 comes this photograph of Mill Road in Pontnewynydd. On the right is Lewis Terrace which has yet to be extended with additional housing. Just behind the bridge, over the coal-polluted Avon Llwyd, is another old building, Osborne Cottage. Still there, the cottage rests at the bottom of Church Lane, leading on to Trevethin.

48. St. Luke's Road with just a horse and trap to disturb the pedestrians. The tall building on the left was built in 1894, and at the time of this photograph belonged to William Wall the local grocer and baker. On the opposite side, the sun blind hangs over the shop of Edwin Rosser the fishmonger and fruiterer. In the background and on the left can be seen Bethany Presbyterian Church, a house of worship which was established in the year 1868. This church fell victim to the demolition contractors in the Spring of 1998.

49. A panoramic view overlooking Pontnewynydd as it appeared just before the outbreak of World War Two in 1939. Taken from Leigh Road, the picture depicts an industrial past showing the extensive works that once created familiar sounds around the town. A few other landmarks from the past may also be seen, such as The Pavilion Cinema, The Western Welsh Garage and the outdoor swimming pool.

50. A view of the mountain from Cwmffrwdoer. Of particular interest is the little halt that used to stand on the line belonging to The Great Western Railway. Built in 1879, this line diverged from Trevethin Junction midway between the stations of Crane Street and Pontnewynydd. The line then continued to Talywain, where it joined The London and North Western Railway branch line which ran from Brynmawr and on through Blaenavon High Level. Passenger services on this line were withdrawn in May 1941.

51. Cwmffrwdoer and Hanbury Road Pontnewynydd, including some interesting features for railway enthusiasts. In the foreground, just to the right of the water column is Branches Fork Shed, a sub depot of Pontypool Road. This shed saw sixty years of service before closing in January 1952. In the background is old Cwmffrwdoer Junior School, another building no longer to be seen. This school provided local children with education from 1881 until 1983.

52. An alternative view of Cwmffrwdoer photographed in about 1938. The chimney stacks belong to Cwmnantddu Brickworks (The Oak Brick Company), which was a reputable manufacturer of fire bricks in days gone by. In the foreground is Kitchener Street on the left, and on the right are Plasycoed Road and Tirpentwys Terrace.

53.   Photographed from Broadway in about 1932 is this view overlooking Park Gardens, towards Penygarn. Looking carefully in the centre it can be seen that the area is still being developed, with houses under construction on Penygarn Hill.

54.   This concluding picture of Chapter Two shows early days at Penygarn Road. The houses in the centre were built here in 1903 and 1904, with those to the left following later. Further up the road, just out of view is the Baptist Chapel, founded in 1727 amidst a period of religious passion. It is recorded that the founders themselves, carried stones recovered from the River Avon Llwyd up the long steep hill to Penygarn to erect their house of worship. The enthusiasm held at Penygarn was to lead the way for a great Baptist ideological following in the valley.

CHAPTER 3

Further Afield

This chapter will deal with some photographic memories of Pontypool's closely allied communities of Griffithstown, Sebastopol and New Inn. It can be said that the suburb of Griffithstown was born at Coed-y-Gric Farm, a late 16th Century homestead, with its small band of workers occupying a few cottages where Bridge Street and the nearby Masons Arms Inn stand today. Pastoral life continued uninterrupted for more than 150 years until the arrival of The Industrial Revolution and a completely re-styled existence to accompany it. First of all came the canal which opened for industrial traffic between Pontnewynydd and Newport in 1796, to be superseded by a more efficient railway system in 1852 with jobs a plenty. Amongst the railway company employees was one Henry Griffiths, a man of innovation and foresight. He quickly identified the forthcoming problems of plenty of work, yet with little provision of adequate housing to complement the situation. Hence, with the help of a couple of local businessmen, Griffiths formed The Pontypool Road Benefit Building Society. Beginning with a plot of land extending from Coed-y-Gric Road to High Street, housing development in the area was energetic, soon satisfying the demand. The name of Henry Griffiths, always at the forefront in these early days of progression, inevitably led to the adoption of his name by the community he had helped to create. The development of the district continued briskly through the latter half of the nineteenth century, with the communities of New Inn and Sebastopol gaining a new-found prosperity. Much of this was due to another mainstay economy to rule the region, that provided by Panteg Steelworks, of which some interesting photographs appear later in this book.

55. A picture of tranquillity looking towards Barretts Bridge which spans over the canal at Griffithstown. The construction of The Monmouthshire Canal followed the passing of an Act Of Parliament in 1792; a section of 11 miles from Pontnewynydd to Newport was opened to traffic in February 1796. There was much anger from the owner of Coed-y-Gric Farm at the time, Mr. Joseph Cowles, he having a number of objections and claims of extensive damage being caused to his farm buildings by the construction of the canal. Protracted court action followed with the farmer winning his case against the Canal Company; seen as an important victory at the time, it was to lead to the building of the bridge over the waterway and further improvements to surrounding structures at this point.

56. This view of the canal is seen some 100 metres from the other side of Barretts Bridge, looking towards Skew Bridge. The houses of Staffordshire Row are seen in the distance. Appropriately named, these houses were originally built to house a number of workers who had moved from the Staffordshire area to Pontypool, all in search of employment at the Lower Mills Works. On the right of this picture a goods train is seen heading in the direction of Pontypool and Blaenavon.

At their Panteg Works

RICHARD THOMAS & BALDWINS

produce

STEEL INGOTS,
BARS AND BILLETS
(MILD STEEL, ALLOY
AND STAINLESS QUALITIES)

STEEL BLACK SHEETS

STAINLESS SHEETS

MERCHANT MILL PRODUCTS:
BARS, ROUNDS, ETC.

Enquiries should be addressed to
RICHARD THOMAS & BALDWINS LTD
Head Office: 47 Park Street, London, W.1
Telephone: Mayfair 8432

R. J. ELMORE

FAMILY BUTCHER

★ **BEST** Meat
. . . . Only

THE HIGHWAY
PONTYPOOL ROAD

Telephone :—GRIFFITHSTOWN 2113

For Finest Value in

GROCERIES & PROVISIONS

Come to us

DANIEL & SON - The Grocers

150 years trading

PONTYPOOL and GRIFFITHSTOWN

57. The Post Office at Griffithstown pictured in 1908. In those days it was situated at premises in Windsor Road, which are presently occupied by Windsors Stores. An earlier Post Office which served the town was sited at No. 66 Commercial Street.

58. This is quite an early view overlooking the Pontypool Union Workhouse (Coed-y-Gric Institution). The busy engine sheds of Pontypool Road are seen, but the houses of Union Lane (Coed-y-Gric Road) and Sunnybank Road have yet to arrive, so changing the scene significantly.

59. More widely recognised in modern times as Panteg Hospital, the premises are seen here in about 1914 whilst still an Institution for the homeless and destitute. Following World War One which had started in 1914, the Institution gradually changed its status to that of a hospital complex. First opening in the year 1837, and despite continued threats of closure for one reason or another, the building still manages to survive, these days offering specialised medical care.

60/61. Both of these photographs were taken at The Institution in 1916, during the height of the war. As will be seen in the upper picture, there was quite a large number of wounded to be cared for; the premises now being used to treat casualties from the battlefields of France and Belgium. Below, the photographer has been allowed into the kitchens, primitive as they were in those days.

62. Bridge Street Griffithstown, with its corner shop 'Bristol House'. This shop was for a number of years occupied by John Daniel and Sons, grocers. Some readers may also remember the family owning another grocery business in Crane Street Pontypool; this store receiving mention in Chapter 8.

63. High Street, and an opportunity to view The Hanbury Hotel in 1905, a period when Mrs. Martha Shenton was the landlady. It was in 1877 when plans were accepted to build a prestigious hostelry on this site. The Hanbury was the important meeting place for members of The Associated Society of Locomotive Engineers and Firemen (ASLEF). The founders were Pontypool Road engine drivers Charles Perry, Evan Evans, Thomas Harding and Tom Roderick in February 1880.

64. With St. Hilda's Church in the background, this leading-road through Griffithstown was at one time believed to have been known as Church Road. These days of course its name has been changed to Greenhill Road and has benefited by a little modernisation since this picture of 1906.

65. This is Broad Street as photographed from The Hanbury Hotel. The imposing building second from the left was the old Police Station, erected here in 1892. On the opposite side of the street, at No. 57, with the canopy, is one of Griffithstown's bespoke tailors, Benjamin Charles Bowen.

66. Windsor Road in 1915, with a period horse and cart parked outside the draper's shop of Francis Edward Jenkins. These were days when almost anything could be purchased in the wide variety of retailers in Griffithstown, without the need to travel to Pontypool or beyond. On the opposite corner, with a sign writer at work, is Herbert James Thomas's grocery and baker's shop. Strangely enough, eighty years on, this particular shop is still a baker's.

67. This time the scene is looking towards the lower end of Windsor Road and the very presence of a photographer has brought just about every child onto the street. Notice the shop on the right belonging to George William Jones, which has a fine display of rabbits for sale; this choice of meat being a latter-day delicacy for the dinner table.

68. A look down Edward Street with part of Charles Street in the background. House-building in Edward Street began in the 1890s although the street was not completed until 1910. This picture is from about 1905 and shows that the left-hand side is only partially completed at this time.

69. Commercial Street with a group of children standing outside The Mechanics' Institute. The masonry used in the construction of this building was retrieved from the then-demolished Pontrhydyrun Station, and kindly donated to the ASLEF organisation for their new premises. Next door to the Institute can be seen the old Wesleyan Methodist Chapel.

70. A fascinating image of what is now Kemys Street, it originally bearing the name High Street. Photographed from the canal bridge in about 1907, the gradient of this street must have presented a gruelling task for the horsedrawn transport of the period.

71. The main street of Sebastopol, South Street. Initially known as Greenhill Road, in 1907 and by public request the name was changed to South Street. The double-fronted business premises is named 'The Bridge Tea Warehouse', an unusual name for an establishment selling ales and strong liquor. The building also housed Sebastopol's first Post Office but, by 1888 it had changed hands again, this time being acquired by the Cardiff based brewery of William Hancock and Company Limited.

72/73. Two views along the canal at Sebastopol. In the upper photograph the large building on the right is The Crown Inn. The original Crown Inn on this site dated from the early 19th Century, although the one seen here, and still there today, was built in 1915. This picture was taken in the 1930s and shows the canal falling into disrepair and neglect through lack of use. The lower photograph, taken some twenty years earlier from the Crown Bridge, shows a G.W.R. dredger at work. The Great Western Railway Company took ownership of the waterway following their acquisition of The Monmouthshire Railway and Canal Company in 1880.

74. Gladstone Place as observed in the year 1912. The six bay-windowed houses on the left were built in 1902, and originally called Colenso Terrace in commemoration of a celebrated battle of the Boer War in South Africa. Gladstone Place was formed by the amalgamation of Colenso Terrace with two other nearby rows of houses, named Tamplin's Terrace and Rowland's Terrace which had been built some years previous. The name Gladstone probably being adopted to honour the name of the country's foremost Prime Minister of Victorian times, William Gladstone.

75. From around 1960 this picture is looking up the hill towards Crown Bridge with a not so busy road. The immediate building on the left is The Post Office with The Crown Inn further along. This scene was pictured a few years before the bridge received yet another badly needed widening and facelift to cope with ever increasing volumes of traffic.

76. The Turnpike when it was the main road junction for Abergavenny and Newport, with an R.A.C. patrolman assisting with traffic control. On the left is the original Toll-House which dated from the 18th Century and held by the Pontypool Turnpike Trust. The collection of tolls from travellers to the town at this point, was the principal means of funding road maintenance in the area. Transferring to private ownership in 1875, this historic building stood the test of time until 1963 when demolition finally took place.

77. Looking down The Jockey Pitch and the design of the few cars on this, the main road from Pontypool to Abergavenny and Usk, suggests the period to be the 1930s. Much has happened since this old picture was taken, with a completely new road system having been constructed at the bottom of the hill.

78. The photographic tour of outer Pontypool continues with a visit to New Inn. The approach road on the left leads to the 'new' Pontypool Road Station, the original buildings being situated on the other side of the bridge. The large house in the centre, at the time of this photograph, belonged to the Burgoyne family, respected builders in the Pontypool district.

79. In the centre of New Inn and all is relatively quiet 90 years ago. The turning to the right, behind the lamppost, was later to be developed as the road to Griffithstown. The first building on the right, No. 121 is advertising itself as Refreshment Rooms, whilst opposite is a sight not seen for a number of years; a load of coal has been delivered onto the main road and awaits the customer's removal to the coal shed!

80. This photograph makes interesting comparison with the one above, with an advancement of some thirty years. The corner on the right has been considerably developed, with Dean's Newsagent's and Tobacconist's having been built.

81. There is no danger in standing in the middle of the road, here at New Inn in 1910. The first building on the left is The Rising Sun Inn which had recently been extensively altered. Next door is an old cottage, since demolished and now the site of the pub's car park. On the opposite side can be seen the entrance to the old coal yard, with the Post Office and Butcher's shop belonging to Edmund Gwatkin, close by.

82. This view looks in the opposite direction from the previous picture and has been taken from The Upper New Inn (now known as The Teazer). The elderly couple on the right (notice that there is no need for a pavement), are stood beside Mary Ann Terrace. The General Stores seen on the opposite side of the road are nowadays the premises of a Launderette with a Veterinary Surgeon next door.

83. A 1930s picture postcard with Griffithstown to be seen in the distance. This picture has been taken from New Road, a road which was constructed during the early 1920s to form a link between New Inn and Griffithstown.

84. There are many photographs included in this book that illustrate scenes which are now forgotten, and the reader will need reminding on occasions where they might be. This is Berry's Corner which has seen a few changes over the years. The white cottages on the left are now gone and the large house, hidden behind the trees is now the New Inn Nursing Home.

CHAPTER 4

Schooldays

85. Pontymoile School during its heyday in 1905. This school was built between 1859 and 1860 by The Ebbw Vale Company, as a mark of the esteem it held for the welfare of its employees and their children. Education was not seen as a priority in the early years of the nineteenth century; knowledge being made available only to those who could afford to pay for it, with no help provided by government. There was little enthusiasm from parents either, particularly when a 7 or 8 year-old child could earn a few shillings working underground, much more useful than being mystified by the 'Three Rs'. Pontymoile School was demolished in 1986, the land having since been transformed by a new road system.

86. Panteg Wern Mixed School, Sebastopol, as it was named when first opened in October 1911 with accommodation for some 400 pupils. Reorganisation by the Education Authority recommended closure in 1976 due to the age of the building; it surviving however for a further five years. A disastrous fire occurred in March 1981 which led to its final demise the following year. The site has since been redeveloped by provision of accommodation for the elderly residents of Sebastopol.

87. A rare photograph from the year 1897 which was taken during the construction of Jones's West Monmouth School For Boys, as it was then known. The foundation stone was laid by Mrs. Hanbury, with the school officially opening in 1898 and catering for a hundred pupils. The huge cost for that time, of £30,000 was met by the accumulated funds of a seventeenth century legacy to a London company - The Worshipful Company Of Haberdashers. The first headmaster was a Mr. J.H. Priestley of Usk Grammar School, his name later being adopted as one of West Mon's house titles.

88. An aerial view of West Mon now showing the new Science Block which had been added in 1934. This extension was to cost some £20,000 and was opened by Mr. H.L. Stephenson, Master of The Worshipful Company Of Haberdashers, the school's benefactors. Accommodation was now available for 600 pupils and the headmastership at the time was in the capable hands of Mr. Ivor Jones, he serving the school for a remarkable 30 years.

89. The First XV at West Mon during the 1968-69 season. Seen left to right the team is made up of the following boys. Back Row - T. Cole, R. May, P. Rees, R. Phillips, D. Davies, A. Dixon and S. Trumper. Middle Row - R. Hewkins, R. Barrell, H. Stockham (Captain), Mr. A. Hodge, M. Davies, G. Price and G. Ball. Front Row - A. Lewis, P. Fraser, C. Gaut and C. Mallet.

Graham Price was of course to go on to earn every honour in the game of rugby, playing for Pontypool R.F.C., Wales, The Barbarians and The British Lions.

90. School photographs are a 'must' and former pupils will ponder over this one. Taken at West Mon's main entrance in the late 1940s or early '50s perhaps, the photograph is centered around Mr. John 'Jim' Moseley. Mr. and Mrs. Moseley will be fondly remembered by many an 'old boy'. As head of the French Department, who could ever forget, Mr. Moseley's supremely polished French accent and his wife's in-depth knowledge of the world of biology.

91. Trevethin Comprehensive School at Penygarn as it is now known. Originating as a Baptist College, the students were subsequently transferred to Cardiff to continue their theological studies in 1893; the lease for the Penygarn building being purchased with the help of local funds to supplement government grants. The new school was to be known as The Pontypool Grammar School For Girls and formerly opened its doors to pupils on January 13th 1897. Commencing with just 43 girls, the numbers were to eventually pass the 600 mark. Throughout its history the school was invariably referred to as 'The County', a reference that was to disappear with its conversion to a Comprehensive School in 1982.

92. The first Headmistress at The County was Miss Dobell, who on appointment to the important position in 1897, was rewarded with an annual salary of £120. Fees for pupils were established at thirty shillings (£1.50) per term, except for a minority who might have been fortunate enough to have earned themselves a free scholarship. The photograph above is an early look at the well presented dining room.

93. A number of improvements and extensions were made to the County School over the years, the gymnasium for one, which was completed in 1939. Here are some members of a netball team in 1954 accompanied by a member of staff. Not all of the names have been traced unfortunately, but those known are Pamela Phillips, Pamela Elliott, Mary Peckham, Joan Pearson, Pat Challenger and Fay Britton.

94. A customary school photograph at The County School in 1957 and this was a year amidst the 'Miss Francis' era. The revered Miss Francis was the school's longest-serving headmistress (1945-1969) and was seen as the role model for the female species. Whilst the above photograph is devoid of names, the girls would now be in their 'young fifties' and will be able to recognise themselves and remember with fondness those delectable green berets and uniforms.

95. George Street School, the building of which dated back to 1847. Having seen a number of improvements and extensions over the years, its long history came to an end with demolition in 1989. This particular photograph is from about 1949, with teachers Mr. James on the left and Mr. Hood on the right. Many of the pupils are known and they include from left to right Front Row - Michael Jeremiah, Master Walden, Myra Jones, Mary Roberts, Pat Keogh, unknown, Kathleen ? , Margaret Owen, Jean Morgan, Danny Packwood and Raymond Smith. Middle Row - Colin Stephens, Tony Goodchild, Ivor Probert, unknown. Back Row - Unknown, Edwin Martin, Ken Holvey, Master Watkins, Master Parker, Master Lear and John Hawkins.

96. Some twenty-plus smiling boys' faces from a class at St. Alban's Roman Catholic School in about 1944. The Headmaster at the time was Mr. M. O'Callaghan.

97. A sunny day in the summer of 1952 and the boys and girls seen here are photographed at Griffithstown Junior School.

98. The teaching staff of St. Alban's Junior School and the ladies seen in this picture are: Back Row - Treena Hitchings, Cathy Clements (Student Teacher), Helen Alldred, Rosemary Jenkins and Gill Price (Nursery Nurse). Front Row - Catherine Johnstone (Deputy Head), Kay Baynham (Head Teacher), Sister Marian Sweeney and Beverley Bannon.

99. A photograph taken of the girl pupils at Twmpath Central School during its first year of activity in 1927. One of the most respected Secondary Modern schools in the Pontypool district, pupil achievement here was consistently at a commendable level. The arrival of comprehensive education in 1982 ultimately saw the amalgamation of Twmpath with West Mon Grammar.

100. Continuing with some photographic records at local schools, it is the turn of New Inn Nursery on this occasion in 1992. Virtually all of the youngsters and teachers names have been traced and they are seen as follows reading left to right. Back Row - Mrs Lewis, Miss Styles, Liam Powell, Alexander Denning, unknown, Owen Fisher, Claire Baker, unknown, Adam Langley, Donna Cole, and Mrs. Vidler (Head Teacher). Third Row - Leannis Hogan, Hannah Godfrey, Karen Gaywood, Sarah Green, unknown, Caryss Powell, Sian G. Evans and Sara Davies. Second Row - Adam Chivers, Rebecca Day, Sophie Thomas, Stephanie Parker, Sarah Bousie, Rachel Perry, Vicki Oliver, Amy Bertarelli, Jenny Jones, Sian E. Evans and Joel Woodward. Front Row - Jonathan Griffiths, Jamie Godfrey, Daniel Godfrey, unknown, James Whelan, Joel Gillard, Jonathan Burt and Ross Picken.

CHAPTER 5

Religious Concerns

101. Probably beginning in the 1970s, there has been a familiar pattern concerning places of worship in the valleys; one of a declining fellowship and subsequent closure. In this chapter will be found a few photographic reminders of former churches and chapels, beginning with St. David's Presbyterian Church as seen above. Situated in Osborne Road, a short distance from The Royal Cinema, St. David's opened for worship in 1905. Well-supported for many years, it eventually closed in April 1991. The building has since been converted into flats.

102. Detailed and precise information relating to the ancestry of Trevethin Church is not plentiful. There is however limited mention in some 13th Century records, suggesting establishment during this period; the church being dedicated to a 6th Century Christian patriarch, Saint Cadoc. Trevethin, previously a dependent chapel of Llanover, achieved separate parochial status in the year 1843. Services at the church were conducted in pure Welsh until a trial period of the English tongue in 1817; this was to last only for a brief spell as the Pontypool Christians of the day, could not, or probably did not, wish to follow the language. Those who could however, worshipped in the private chapel attached to Pontypool Park until St. James's opened in Hanbury Road in 1821, thereby catering permanently for their linguistic needs.

103. Trevethin Vicarage, as pictured in about 1908. St. Cadoc's first incumbent was Reverend Thomas Davies and amongst his achievements whilst in service, were splendid enlargements to his church and the building of a parsonage. This original building was later to become one of conflicting interests, namely The Masons Arms public house! The new vicarage as seen above emanates from the nineteenth century.

104. Holy Communion is given to some school leavers of St. Alban's Catholic School in 1944. A number of the pupils' names have been recollected as follows - Stan Cotteral, John Askew, Ivor Snooks, George Lankshear, Cliff Stone, Pearl Bayliss, Joyce Hewitt, unknown, unknown, Margaret Bush, Margaret Lewis, Cyril Daley, John Edwards, Doreen Hayes, Margaret Regan, Georgina Smith, Mary Regan and seated are Ralph Trehearne, Ray Burchell and Victor Russell.

105. The ancient church of Mamhilad, the major part of which dates back more than 600 years and there are a number of interesting features to be found here. Entrance to the building by foot, is over a horizontally-placed gravestone to the memory of one Aaron Morris who died in the year 1680. Other remains to be found in the west gallery are fragments of a screen, with traceried panels, which also dates from Mediaeval times.

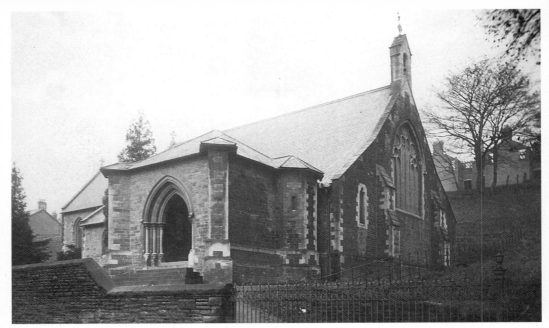

106. St. Luke's Church at Pontnewynydd, yet another religious establishment whose doors are now closed. The building, seen here in Edwardian times was consecrated in 1879, having been redesigned and rebuilt on the same site as an earlier and smaller church. The interior of this newer building was particularly attractive, yet unfortunately funds have not come forth to preserve St. Luke's.

107. Ebenezer Chapel Cwmffrwdoer with a collection of ornate 19th Century memorials. This ancient place of worship, which was opened in 1742 is one of the oldest in the district and still survives to this day and known as Ebenezer United Reformed Church.

108. The Wesleyan Chapel as it once appeared in the centre of Pontnewynydd, with Zion Hill on the right. This chapel was opened in 1849 and enjoyed a dedicated Methodist following, until a disastrous fire almost destroyed the building on July 4th 1989. Also seen in this picture is another former significant landmark, the cast-iron drinking fountain.

109. On the left is a photograph taken on the steps of Park Terrace Primitive Methodist Church in June 1906. The gentleman with the top hat is Dr Francis Clark from the State of Indiana, U.S.A. who was the founder of the Christian Endeavour movement. The early years of the 20th Century brought a period of great religious revival throughout Wales, and the visit of Dr Clark to Pontypool was, at the time, deemed to be a great honour. Opening for worship in 1878, Park Terrace church attracted large and enthusiastic congregations until the early 1970s. As reported so often, those congregations dwindled to unsustainable numbers and the decision was taken to close the building and merge with the nearby chapel in Nicholas Street. Park Terrace church was pulled down in 1983 and has now been replaced by housing.

110. A scarce photograph of the original Wesleyan Methodist Church which stood in Crumlin Street Pontypool. This church was built in the year 1814 to accommodate 200 worshippers. As the years went by, the congregation's size outgrew that of the Crumlin Street premises and the members moved to a vacated Mount Pleasant Church in Nicholas Street in 1909. The original church has long since been demolished but visitors to Nicholas Street will still find a warm welcome there.

111. The stately-looking St. Hilda's Church in Griffithstown, seen here in 1906. St. Hilda's was consecrated on 6th March 1888, with the adjacent Church Hall being added in 1896; further extensions to this, taking place between 1912 and 1913. Prior to the opening of the church in 1888, local followers of the established church spent some five years holding their services in numerous surrounding buildings. Land at the site in Griffithstown was eventually donated by Mr. J.C. Hanbury of Pontypool, the actual construction taking some eighteen months to complete.

112. St. Hilda's Vicarage as seen at the turn of the twentieth century, this quite early photograph showing that Sunnybank Road has yet to be fully developed. St. Hilda's first vicar was Reverend J.E. Dunn and it was he who was instrumental in the recognition of Griffithstown as a parish in its own right.

113. At the corner of Oxford Street and Kemys Street in Griffithstown stands the Congregational Church, still surviving after more than a century of history. This particular photograph is from about 1920, the church having established itself some thirty-five years earlier. The initial foundation stone was laid in May 1885 by Mr. William Sandbrook, with the basement which housed the schoolroom, being completed the following November. Thanks to the skills of local builder John Burgoyne and some devoted labour from the church members, the finished building was opened on April 11th 1886.

114. The Wesleyan Methodist Church at New Inn, pictured here in its original design and appearance at the time of inauguration in December 1909. Visitors today will know that an additional church building now stands alongside the original structure, which is currently used as an infant play-centre.

CHAPTER 6

Buildings of Historic Interest

115. One of Pontypool's most noted landmarks is The Folly, a structure dating from the eighteenth century. This scene which also includes some nearby cottages, is from about 1902, when The Folly was owned by the eminent Hanbury family. The tower, being such a prominent attraction and guide to enemy aircraft during World War Two, was demolished and it was almost fifty years before action was taken to restore it to its former glory.

116/117. The Bandstand in the park at Pontypool, which was erected to the memory of Sidney Tudor Roderick (1868-1929). Sidney Roderick was probably the town's greatest musician and led the Pontypool Band for more than forty years. As a composer his work was revered well beyond the boundaries of Pontypool. This photograph shows the bandstand nearing completion in readiness for the official opening by Mr. Arthur James J.P, C.C. on July 30th 1931. The lower photograph shows the forty-plus members of The Battalion Band during the early 1900s. Their leader Mr. Roderick, is seen fifth from the right in the centre of the picture.

118. The splendour of Pontypool Park House, seen in days whilst still the mansion belonging to the Hanbury dynasty. Built in the late 17th Century for Major John Hanbury, it was to see a number of extensions and improvements before eventual acquisition by a Holy Order in 1914. In subsequent years the house was further developed, and with the addition of more modern buildings, was to become St. Alban's Comprehensive School.

119. Another prominent listed landmark overlooking Pontypool is The Grotto, built sometime between 1830 and 1846 as a summer retreat for members of the Hanbury family. Seen here in about 1925, the building was always a popular attraction to sightseers but was unfortunately allowed to fall into decay. Again however, it was a structure to rise from the ashes, finally to be restored in 1997. It has won national praise from The Royal Institution of Chartered surveyors, as one of the country's finest examples of small scale conservation.

120.   The National Health Service was formed in 1948, with the guidance and dynamism of that stalwart politician Aneurin Bevan, Minister of Health and M.P. for the nearby constituency of Ebbw Vale. Prior to this event, patient-care and hospital facilities relied entirely on voluntary finance from the public sector. The first ideas for a hospital to serve the Pontypool district were mooted in the year 1900, and robust campaigning among local industrialists brought an enthusiastic response. Workers needed little convincing that a voluntary contribution of just one penny a week would secure all their health requirements. Employers too played their part with an agreement to add a further contribution equalling 25% of their workers' donations. An official committee was formed and a site chosen at Leigh Road, on land given by Mr. John Capel Hanbury. The building contract was awarded to the Pontnewynydd firm of Bailey Brothers, their tender of £6384 being accepted. Thus the hospital was completed and officially opened by Mrs. Hanbury on October 19th 1903. The scheme was an enormous success but with initial facilities of just 19 beds and 3 cots, there was soon a need for expansion. Numerous such expansions appeared over the years and the photograph above, from 1928, was taken during the addition of a three-storey wing. This provided a further 21 beds and as the signs show, local firms Lougher the architects and William Arthur the builders completed the task. The cost, some £20,000 and void of any government assistance, was again met by voluntary contribution with a generous and welcomed donation from the Miners' Welfare Fund.

The hospital continued to serve the community until the early 1990s, by which time it was considered to be antiquated and too costly to maintain. The building, with its 'castle-like' appearance is now completely closed and 90 years of sterling service has come to an end.

Matron P. A. EBDON

who was appointed Matron of the Pontypool and District Hospital in 1931. Trained at the East Suffolk and Ipswich Hospital, Miss Ebdon served at the Royal Hants Hospital, Winchester, and the Royal Gwent Hospital, Newport, before coming to Pontypool.

121. The former nurses' home which once served the Pontypool and District Hospital. The home is seen here shortly after its official opening by Mrs. W.P. James in October 1915. The home was further extended to cater for increased numbers of staff and opened for use in June 1931. Unfortunately, as with the hospital itself, this building is also now closed and faces an uncertain future.

122. An unusually early photograph which was taken in one of the hospital wards during Christmas 1910. The ward is probably the new extension which was opened in July of that year. This was known as Capel Wing, so named in memory of Capel Hanbury, Mr J.C. Hanbury's son and heir who died in 1908 at the tender age of fourteen.

123. Before the Industrial Revolution reached Pontypool, the district was abundant with farms and agricultural land; the scene above is at Church Farm Trevethin in 1907. This ancient farm was built around 1645 and, in 1997 earned the accolade of a Grade 2 listed building. The present owner, Mr. John Jeremiah is to be congratulated on the fine preservation of this 17th Century example of Pontypool farming architecture.

124. The Canal Junction Cottage at Pontymoile in about 1900, another listed building of historical significance and interest. This area was the important junction of two canals, The Monmouthshire and The Brecknock and Abergavenny. On this photograph the old lifting winch is seen still in place.

125. An early picture which shows three essential buildings in the centre of Pontypool. To the left is St. James's Church which was consecrated in the year 1821. This church was strongly supported in the early days by the English immigrant worshippers, who were experiencing difficulties with the Welsh-only services being conducted at Trevethin. In the centre is the Town Hall which opened in 1856, the building also incorporating the magistrates court and council offices. Just to the side of the Town Hall can be seen the County Constabulary Offices, housing Pontypool's Police Force until the modern and much enlarged premises were built in the early 1960s.

126. A picture of the former Municipal Buildings, Glantorfaen House in Commercial Street some forty years ago. The building these days is occupied by a firm of local solicitors, Messrs. Watkins and Gunn.

127. An exceptionally early view of Pontypool's Library. This important amenity was opened to the public on September 21st 1908, and is pictured here a few days before the event. Workmen are seen in the process of putting the final touches to the building. The cost of this enterprise was met by funds from the Carnegie Trust, the conception of that great Scottish philanthropist Andrew Carnegie, who contributed so much to the peoples' needs in the valleys at the turn of the last century.

128. A gentleman poses outside the decoratively built Board Room belonging to the Pontypool Union Workhouse; the stonework indicating the year of the building as 1899. The structure of course will be more familiarly referred to as Panteg Hospital. This picture obviously pre-dates the major extensions that led to gradual and progressive conversion from a workhouse for the destitute, to a popular hospital.

129. Following the armistice which brought The Great War to an end in November 1918, the mood of the country called for nationwide memorials to the fallen. The site chosen for Pontypool was the entrance to the park, the scheme being led by local J.P. Mr. Godfrey James. Eventually costing some £900, the Pontypool and Abersychan Joint Memorial Gates were dedicated on August 4th 1924. Tablets bearing the names of those lost in the war, were then completed and unveiled by Major-General Lord Treowen on December 18th 1924. The names of further losses from World War Two and Korea were added in more recent years. The total loss of life remembered on this memorial amounts to well over 600!

130. At the entrance to Panteg Cemetery stands the cenotaph honouring the district's war heroes. This memorial was unveiled on Sunday November 27th 1921 by local veteran Quartermaster Sergeant Major T.H. Humphreys R.A.
Local builders Thomas Jones and Son of Pontypool built the monument, and an enthusiastic crowd of more than 1200 attended the unveiling ceremony; the war had been over for three years but the huge feeling of sorrow for the loss of life lingered on. The names of more than 150 local warriors are inscribed on the memorial.

131. Barretts Bridge Griffithstown, and on the right is the 16th century Coed-y-Gric Farm. This farm was the centre of a small community 400 years ago, consisting of just a few nearby cottages. One of these, was many years later to become The Masons Arms public house, mention of which begins to appear in documents dating from 1852. This public house was to enjoy great popularity through the nineteenth century with the arrival of the nearby railway workings. An early landlady, one Mrs Lewis, was said to have the need to send her weekly takings to the bank at Pontypool in a wheelbarrow, so good was business!

132. Panteg House as it looked in 1910. Originally it was known as 'Belvedere', the home of Mr Isaac Butler, manager of the hammering and finishing department at Panteg Works. The house has had a chequered history, ranging from a Belgian refugee centre, a military hospital and a popular local social club.

CHAPTER 7

Sports, Special Events & Entertainment

133. D. 'Ponty' Jones as he appears on a rare autographed postcard. David Phillip Jones was captain of Pontypool R.F.C. for three seasons from 1904 to 1907. Born in the town in 1882, he gained a Welsh Cap whilst playing on the wing in 1907 and also played for London Welsh. His brothers J.P. (Jack) and J.P. (Tuan) were also noted players at the time. The legendary 'Ponty' Jones died at the early age of 54 and is buried at Llanfrechfa churchyard.

Cyril Sharp

SPORTS
OUTFITTER

**42, George Street,
PONTYPOOL**

134. A picture from the 1932-33 season of Pontypool R.F.C., the results for the season being - Played 45, Won 25, Drew 5, Lost 15, Points For 386, Against 169. The previous season they had secured the Welsh championship. The gentlemen seen here are, Left to Right Back Row: Joe Williams (Committee), J. Evans (Committee), E. Donovan, A.H. Allen, F. Elias, G.H. Head (Committee), G. Garnett and Ivor Jones. Middle: W. Vallis (Committee), E. Bolter, J.A. Bowen, G. Harvey, R. Belcher, W. Gough, C. James, J. Atkins, J. Jones (Trainer). Front: F.J. Morris, J.T. Bodger, Gwyn Bayliss (Vice Captain), Arthur James (Chairman), Cliff Axford (Captain), W.R. Meredith (Secretary), G.J. Newey, Horace Turner and Don Cormack. Seated: F.J. Bowyer and Ivor Silcox.

135. The Pontypool XV pictured during their ambitious French tour of 1910. The photograph was taken just before they met the champions Bordeaux in February of that year. The journey to France in those days was a long one by boat and train and perhaps the two-day trek took its toll; the Frenchmen were the narrowest of victors by 5 points to 3.

136. A Pontypool United team of yesteryear and here are some names to remember. Back Row: Bobby Malsom, Don Jenkins, David Games, Lionel Watkins and Paul Rosser. Middle: David Leighfield, Ron Matthews, Colin Williams, John Stanley, Harry Vaux, Mike Williams and John Harris. Front: Benny Jones, Malcolm Roynon and Howard Jackson.

137. The Pontypool Youth R.F.C. Invincible Team of 1969-1970 and here are the names to remember, seen left to right. Back Row: Laurie Daniel (Coach), Jeremy Mayers, Ralph Bendall, Steve Jones, Shane Taylor and Derek Parry. Middle Row: Bill Smith, Steve Casey, Michael Othen, Paul Green, Richard Phillips, Carl Jones and Graham Sherwood. Front Row: Ronald Taylor, Alan Jones, Steve Jeffries, Wayne Preston, Fred Howells, Ian Ross and unknown. Incidentially, the team also proved to be invincible during the following season 1970-1971.

138. The St. Hilda's Griffithstown Church Lads Brigade Company who retained the Football and Sports Challenge Cup at Southerndown camp in 1920. Lt. Colonel Harold Griffiths was second in command of the camp and the vicar of Griffithstown, Reverend H.O. Davies was Staff Chaplain.

139. Trevethin Church Cricket Club in 1934. In the back row are, E. Newport (Umpire), A. Saxon, A. Timms, D. Robinson, G. Higton, Major Hamer Lewis, S. Fawdry, W. Higton, T. Johns, W. Phillips, B. Rees (Committee) and W. Phillips (Scorer). Seated: C.Phillips (Vice Captain) and D. Higton (Captain). Front Row Standing: H.E. Bishop (Committee), W.C. Haydon (Vice-President), W. Callender (Treasurer), A. Davies (Vice-President), Canon Vaughan W.T. Rees (Vicar), E.W. Moseley (Chairman), J. Ireland (Vice Chairman) and Rev. E.A.M. Cape (Curate). Seated at the front is Mr. T.B. Pearson (Club President) who donated the building to the club and performed the official opening on 26th May 1934.

140. Here are two teams from Trevethin Cricket Club, the First and Second Eleven in 1951. Amongst the group, a few of the players have been traced and some names to remember include W. Hopkins (Umpire), Dr. J.B. Fitzsimons, A. Pinney, O.F. Witty, F. Hagger, M. Fawdry (Scorer), R.R. West (Secretary), S.R. Fawdry, A. Griffiths, N.W.J. Thorne (Captain 1st XI), E.W. Moseley (Vice-President), J.H. Moseley (Chairman), K. Smith, D. Harrhy and L.P. Williams (Vice-Captain 1st XI).

141. There are those who will remark that golf is not a sport but more a way of life. Whatever the view, this way of life has been active in Pontypool since 1903, when a number of prosperous residents decided to form the town's first club. This consisted of a nine-hole course on land near The Tranch, although only to last for four years because of poor terrain. A new 'nine-holer' was then built at New Inn, this remaining in use until 1923 when the new 18-hole course was opened at Trevethin. The 1903 Membership Fees of £1.05 per annum will remind today's golfers of the powers of inflation. The photograph above is probably of the first clubhouse on the present site at Trevethin.

142. Some ex-captains and club officers pictured at the Golf Club during the Golden Jubilee celebrations in 1953. Left to right, they are: Standing - E.E. Williams, H. Russell, J.K. Jones and K.G.S. Gunn. Seated: Mel Jones (Hon. Sec.), L.J. Davies (Captain), H.H. Watkins (President) and R.Lester (Late Pro.). These days there are 600 members and the present clubhouse, which was built in 1976, has had some £100,000 spent on refurbishment. The Club's President is Mr. Glyn Davies, Captain is Ewart Pryer with Jim Howard as professional. The Secretary is Mr. Peter Jones.

143. Past swimmers may now need to be reminded of the whereabouts of this outdoor swimming pool. The pool was at Pontnewynydd and was built by the old Abersychan Urban District Council in the year 1915. The advent of indoor leisure facilities at Pontypool Park have superseded the former pools at Pontnewynydd and Griffithstown.

144. A more up-to-date picture of some enthusiastic swimmers at Pontypool Leisure Centre and the girls include, Back Row: Nicky Pinch, Emma Knott and Maria James. Middle - Angela Smithey, Claire Walbyoff, Hayley Arnold, Jackie Gwillim and Vicky Haines. Front - Tina Charles.

145. The senior and junior athletic champions of Twmpath School in about 1956. The names to match the faces, left to right are, John Gould, John Griffiths, Tony Tomboline, Ms. Wilkie, Maureen Newman and Margaret Owen. John Griffiths was later to play for the Pontypool Rugby Welsh Championship team in 1958-59; then later in the season left to join Hunslet Rugby League Club.

146. The sporting topic featured here is that of Table Tennis and the players are all members of staff of the former Fowler's store. Amongst those to be seen are, Back Row: Ken Betts, Eddie Thomas, Ken Jones and Bob Sweeting. Front: Richard Webb, Harold Gregory, Frank Goodland, Herbert Tibbs, Bill Norman, Cliff Williams, Hazel Tovey, Colin Telfer and Wendy Warman. The date of this picture is about 1957.

147. The Armistice Day Service has been an annual memorial to the victims of war since 1919, and traditionally held on a Sunday morning which falls nearest to November 11th. This photograph, from the 1950s, shows St. James's Church members and the public gathered opposite the Park Gates Memorial.

148. Another scene from a Pontypool district Remembrance Day. This picture shows a group of St. Mary's Panteg Cubs in 1960 stood where the Riverside Estate is today, and a few names are: T. Cole, I. Tweedle, S. Goodland, D. Molloy, I. Trumper, J. Evans and R. Rice.

149. It is some time since such an intricate feat as this was staged in Pontypool. The scene is at an annual Whitsuntide Fête held at The Polo Grounds in 1907, and the performer is a gentleman by the name of 'Daredevil Schreyer'. He propelled himself by bicycle down the specially constructed gradient seen here, then left the machine in mid-air intending to land in a small tank of water. Unfortunately on this occasion, luck or judgement did not prevail and he scraped the side of the target, injuring himself considerably. Looking carefully, just above the tree in the centre, Schreyer can just be seen leaving the bicycle on his way to a dramatic end.

150. The Drinking Fountain which was originally sited by the Town Hall and St. James's Church and erected by Mrs Hanbury Leigh. It was completed and opened for public use on January 17th 1860, and this photograph was taken on a celebratory occasion a few years later. This piece of elaborate Pontypool architecture was removed some years ago.

151. The first Town Bridge which crossed the Avon Llwyd at the bottom of Penygarn Hill was constructed in the middle of the eighteenth century. The photograph above was taken at the opening of the new bridge on August 2nd 1924, the ceremony being led by Major General Lord Treowen C.B., Lord Lieutenant of the County. Making a speech here is Mr. David Udell, Chairman of Pontypool Council, with Lord Treowen to his right, sporting a top hat.

152.   The National Eisteddfod came to Pontypool in August 1924, attracting huge crowds and numerous personalities of the day; none more famous perhaps than H.R.H. The Prince Of Wales, seen here with the a bowler hat and delivering a speech. He was of course to visit the town again in 1936 as King Edward VIII, amidst the crises of massive unemployment and the 'Mrs. Simpson situation.' Also on this picture are Lord Treowen with his traditional top hat and Mr. David Udell to the Prince's left.

153.   This is a group of local ladies participating in the Eisteddfod in 1924 and a few of their names can be recollected as follows - First three on the left, Mrs Walden (Cafe on the Cross), Mrs Tom Edwards, Miss Morris (School Mistress), with 4th and 2nd from the right being Mrs Howell Williams (wife of Rev.Williams, St. David's Hall) and Mrs James (wife of the manager of the Midland Bank).

154. Amateur dramatic societies have always attracted a strong following in the district and on stage here in about 1950 are 'The Resettlement Players'. Regrettably the author has not been able to trace the artistes' names other than Mr. Bill Knight and Mary Knight who are 3rd and 5th from the left, respectively.

155. Social activities were always encouraged for the staff of Fowler's and here is a group photograph from the company's Amateur Dramatic Society. The cast, consisting of a vicar, school staff and pupils are gathered at St. Hilda's Hall Griffithstown in 1956. Most of the names are known and apologies are given to those whom the author has been unable to identify. Left to right, Back Row: Cliff Gordon, Dot Parry, Ron Gray, Yvonne Brown, Mary Surridge, Herbert Tibbs and Frank Goodland. Middle: Unknown and Doug Morris. Front: Unknown, Hazel Tovey, Cliff Williams and Ken Betts.

CHAPTER 8

Trading Places

156. The once-substantial General Post Office and Telephone Exchange which served the area, is pictured in 1906 when Mr William Richards was the town's postmaster. The first office for handling mail was opened in Caroline Street (now Commercial Street) in 1827. The introduction of a 'Penny Post' in 1840 saw a huge increase in demand for communication throughout the country, for those who could read and write in those days. Large Post Offices as seen here, were important buildings in the towns. That trend has now reversed and Pontypool's Office has moved next door, with a Building Society having taken over the original premises.

157. There must be a number of readers of this book who can remember this little shop, and also peering through the window at the craftsman busy at work. This was the watchmaker and jeweller's E. Bryant which used to be situated beneath the Royal Cinema in Osborne Road. Mr Ernest Bryant who is seen on the right with his flat cap, worked as a watchmaker for an incredible 49 years before finally retiring in 1960 at the age of 75.

Broad Street, BLAENAVON,
3 George Street,   The Arcade.
PONTYPOOL,   ABERTILLERY.

M..

Bought of **A. ALLMARK,**

Watches, Clocks and Jewellery.

A Solid Gold Keeper presented to Purchasers of our Gold Wedding Rings.

A CHOICE SELECTION OF SILVER and ELECTRO-PLATED ARTICLES.

FIRST-CLASS REPAIRS, ELECTRO-PLATING & RE-GILDING HIGH GRADE WATCHES AT ALL PRICES.

158. Before the appearance of supermarkets in Pontypool, the shop seen here was one of the most popular grocery stores in the town. It was the shop of John Daniel and Son at Number 7 Crane Street. The staff are seen stood on the doorstep of the store as it looked in the year 1904.

159. A unique view of the upper part of Crane Street, just above the old railway bridge, dating from the 1880s. The first shop on the left was John Littlehales the pork butcher and nearby, with harnesses on display was Truman's the saddlers. To the right is the Montague Hotel, formerly The Crosskeys. These buildings were demolished some years ago and this part of Crane Street is totally unrecognisable these days.

160. The largest shop of its kind in Pontypool was Fowler's Lion House, which stood on the corner of Commercial Street and Crane Street. This picture dates from 1909 and above the lamp, just out of view, was an ornamental lion; this was a remnant from the very early days of the premises when they were part of The Lion Hotel. Founded in the early part of the nineteenth century, the family business served the community for 150 years, through a succession of Fowler sons, the last being E. Worton Fowler. Past customers may also remember 'Top Fowlers' on the corner of Crane Street and Market Street. This was known as Manchester House, and though owned by the Fowler family, was treated as a separate concern to Lion House.

161. Former customers of 'Bottom Fowlers' may recognise some of the friendly female staff seen here in about 1959. Left to right they are, Miss Cooper, Hazel Bendon, Unknown, Ann Chapman, Barbara Wood, Pat Collins and Beryl Pritchard.

162. From the year 1956, the familiar Fowler's delivery van with two members of staff - Colin Telfer (furnishing) and Ken Jones (head window-dresser).

163. From the earliest days of the formation of the Fowler Company, staff recreation and welfare was a prime consideration. Above is a photograph taken on the annual staff outing in July 1960. The venue on this occasion was a visit to the Cheddar Caves.

164. It will not be easy for anyone to picture where the National Provincial Bank was in Pontypool. It used to stand on the corner of George Street, opposite The Crown Hotel (now Woolworths). Many years after this photograph was taken, part of the building became the Quality Cleaners which may be easier to remember. The premises were of course subsequently demolished to allow the badly needed widening of George Street. The manager of the bank at the time of this photograph was Mr. W. Gower Griffiths, possibly the gentleman stood on the left.

165. Some past traders at the bottom of Crane Street are seen here. On the left is Walker's Coffee Tavern, whose proprietor Mr. John Walker also owned the nearby Waverley Hotel. Next to the Coffee Tavern was T.A. Jones the hairdressers and tobacconists. Mr. Jones was also a town councillor for a number of years and faithful servant of St. James's church. Although the appearance of these shops has changed somewhat, the Coffee Tavern building is still there and is currently a Fish Bar and Restaurant.

166. A horse and trap stands outside The Clarence Hotel in 1909. The hotel was strategically placed at the entrance to Pontypool, once a focal point with a 200-year old history behind it. Regrettably however, times have changed, the hotel is no longer.

167. It is possible that one might have had to frequent a public house or two in the Pontypool district to remember some of these business folk. They form a group of publicans belonging to the Pontypool Licensed Victuallers Association and are pictured at the Guinness Brewery during a visit in August 1958.

168. Lots of public houses will have a particular nickname attached to them and the hostelry seen above was known as 'The Tump'. It is of course The Prince of Wales at Cwmynyscoy. The photograph is from about 1930 and in the doorway is stood Mr. W.E. Derrick, landlord at that time.

169. The familiar thatched roof which betrays the identity of this ancient inn, The Horse and Jockey at Usk Road. The period is 1905 when Mr. W.H. Fletcher was the landlord. This public house, on the outskirts of town, was a most popular stopping place for members of the farming community whilst on their way to Pontypool Market. The tranquil scene here illustrates well, the quiet life of long ago.

170/171. Above is a picture of the well-decorated pub, The Unicorn Inn, in Albion Road. The proprietor George Spencer is seen on the left with his sleeves rolled up in 1906. The lower photograph, taken a year later, shows members of the Unicorn Outing Club outside The Old Swan Inn, Almondsbury Bristol. It is hard to imagine the length of time that these horse-drawn charabancs took to get as far as Bristol and back! Possibly in those days, a ferry might have been available to cross the River Severn, thus avoiding the arduous journey through Gloucestershire.

172. The majestic-looking Crown Hotel pictured shortly after the extensive alterations of 1895. The original building dated back to the early years of the nineteenth century and today's residents will need to be reminded of its whereabouts. Nowadays, part of the building is occupied by a branch of Woolworth's store in George Street.

173. A period scene in Hill Street Pontnewynydd. Three old businesses are seen here, Francis Pearce the bootmaker, William Lewis (Liverpool Exchange) a grocer and draper, and The Masons Arms public house with Mr David Samuel the landlord of the day.

CHAPTER 9

Industrial Life

174. What will be a familiar sight to many former miners of the area is the pithead at Tirpentwys. This colliery was sunk in 1878 in the Gellydeg Valley above Cwmffrwdoer, and in its heyday provided up to 1500 jobs. It was to have numerous owners and names over the years, the last, before the 1947 nationalisation, being Tirpentwys Black Vein Steam Coal and Coke Company. Coal production ceased here in the late 1960s.

175. A photograph of some rarity from about 1910, bearing in mind the type of photographic equipment that was available at the time. The scene is at pit bottom Tirpentwys, where a few years earlier a freak accident had taken place. Eight men and boys were killed when the winding rope snapped, whilst hauling the cage to the surface at the end of their shift.

176. Another former colliery of Pontypool which kept a number of men at work over the years. This is Gwenallt Colliery, also known as The Jack Pit and was situated at Cwmffrwdoer. There is little, if any trace of the site these days, the pit being finally de-commissioned on October 5th 1952.

177. This is a scene of industrial life at Blaendare in the 1890s, with a unique opportunity to recall the enterprises of The Blaendare Company Limited. In the distance can be seen the workings of the fire clay brick works and the old colliery (slope). The mountain drift at Blaendare was at one time owned by the engineering and foundry group, Guest, Keen and Nettlefold, and used for extracting the clay for manufacture of fire bricks. Clay extraction ceased in about 1968 and the mine reverted to coal production with open-cast workings to follow.

178. The Crumlin Valley's Colliery at nearby Hafodyrynys. Whilst there had been coal workings here since 1878, the Hafodyrynys pit was not fully sunk and developed until 1914. This was the zenith of coal production in the South Wales coalfield, with an annual production of 57 million tons. Hafodyrynys played an important part in linking the workings of nearby Glyntillery and Tirpentwys during the 1950s. Although Hafodyrynys was closed in 1966, the area was used as a processing (washery) plant for other local collieries until the 1970s.

179. A group of workers identifying themselves as from No.8 Mill, Pontnewynydd, October 1905. Registered as the Pontnewynydd Sheet and Galvanising Company, the works were acquired in 1920 by the well-known company of Partridge, Jones and John Paton Ltd. The sight and sounds of Pontnewynydd Forge were essentially a part of the way of life for local residents, until the emergence of Llanwern Steelworks in the 1960s; this eventually leading to the closure of smaller operations such as Pontnewynydd.

180. Another group photograph from the days at Pontnewynydd Works. This is of a party of workers from the plant and they are seen in about 1945. Amongst the crowd are, Reg Jones, Mr. Dadge, Tom Porter, Bill Atkins, Frank Houston, William Owen, Reg Lilly, J. Waites, Dick and Derrick Brians.

181/182. Pontypool Town Forge, which once operated at the rear of Osborne Road, alongside the Avon Llwyd river. The works dated back to 1830 when it replaced the old plating mill. The forge was to produce high quality iron for the subsequent manufacture of tinplate until about 1884. Then came the revolutionary discoveries of Gilchrist Thomas at nearby Blaenavon, which brought forth the wonders of steel-making and the redundancy of iron. The upper photograph dates from 1900, when the site was a tin works and registered as the Pontypool Works Limited; but by 1920, as with Pontnewynydd, it was amalgamated with Messrs. P. J. and J.P. The picture on the left was taken at the tin works in about 1920, and three of the gentlemen's names can be recalled. Centre, back row is Mr. Parry and in the front are Mr. Hillier (left) and Mr. Micah Lewis. Mr Lewis, amongst other things, was a veteran soldier, a founder member of Pontypool Ex Servicemen's Club and head packer at the Town Forge for 30 years.

183. The large and long-established Panteg Works as it appeared in 1907, a period when it was known as Baldwins Limited. The Baldwin name came through the amalgamation in 1902 of two companies, Messrs. Wright, Butler and Co. and Alfred Baldwin Ltd. Baldwin had already formed a tinplate works near this site in 1885. The works seen above were first founded in 1873 by Sampson Copestake, a London-based silk merchant, who envisaged a fortune to be made in the new steelmaking processes of Monmouthshire.

184. Another old view taken from the canal bridge in Kemys Street Griffithstown, showing the close proximity of Panteg railway station and the works. The station's main building seen here on the left, still stands and is now used as commercial construction premises. The scene on this photograph dates back to about 1908.

185. A group of workers being photographed at Panteg Works whilst it was still in the hands of Baldwins Limited. Panteg has provided employment in the district for more than a century and has survived, despite all the mixed fortunes of the British steel industry. In 1947 it was absorbed by the RTB Group (Richard Thomas and Baldwin) and twenty years later was nationalised, as part of the British Steel Corporation, then concentrating on the manufacture of stainless steel. The 1990s brought further change with re-privatisation and the formation of a new Swedish-based company, Avesta Sheffield Ltd.

186. Mamhilad in the early 1950s. When the war ended in 1945, there was an urgency to attract new industries and work to the area. A joint venture between the chemical group I.C.I. and textile manufacturers Courtaulds was established as early as 1940, to develop a new wonder fibre, 'Nylon'. The new company, to be known as British Nylon Spinners chose a 112-acre site at Pontypool, opening in April 1948. In 1965 the plant became known as I.C.I. Fibres Ltd. and in the golden years provided some 7500 jobs for the area. As so often repeated throughout British industry, the words recession, merger and takeover have affected this once-huge employer. The size of the operation at Mamhilad is but a fraction of what it was, it now being part of the Dupont group with a workforce of less than 200!

187. The cost and supply of water attracts a certain amount of conversation these days. This photograph shows progress in the building of Llandegveth Reservoir in the 1960s. Eventually opening in 1966, the statistics for this project make interesting reading. The lake area absorbed 434 acres of land and now measures $1^1/2$ miles in length and one mile wide. When full the capacity is 5,300 million gallons of water and is part of a scheme providing an average daily supply of 40 million gallons to the homes and industries of south east Wales.

CHAPTER 10

Railway Memories

TRAINS TO LONDON
(PADDINGTON)

SATURDAY MORNINGS

18th JUNE to 10th SEPTEMBER (inclusive)

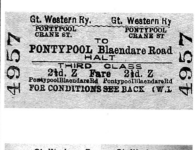

FROM	AS FROM NEWPORT			
	Train No. A02		Train No. A29	Train No. A40
	Depart	Depart	Depart	Depart
	a.m.	a.m.	a.m.	a.m.
BLAENAVON (L.L.)	6 15	—	7 55	9 0
CWMAVON (Mon.) HALT ...	6 20	—	8 1	9 6
CWMFFRWD HALT ...	6 25	—	8 5	9 11
ABERSYCHAN (L.L.)	6 27	—	8 8	9 13
PONTNEWYNYDD	6 31	—	8 11	9 16
PONTYPOOL (Crane Street)	6 35	—	8 16	9 21
PONTYPOOL (Blaendare Rd.) HALT	6 38	—	8 18	9 23
PANTEG & GRIFFITHSTOWN	6 42	—	8 22	9 27
SEBASTOPOL	6 44	—	8 24	9 29
PONTRHYDYRUN HALT ...	6 46	—	8 26	9 31
UPPER PONTNEWYDD ...	6 48	—	8 28	9 33
CWMBRAN	6 52	—	8 31	9 37
LLANTARNAM	6 55	—	8 35	9 41
PONTHIR	6 58	—	8 38	9 44
CAERLEON	7 2	—	8 42	9 48
NEWPORT ... ...arrive	7 9	—	8 51	9 54

Note against Train No. A40 column: Runs 2nd July to 27th August inclusive

Note against rows bracketed E

188. An extract from a British Railways Western Region timetable of 1960, giving details of the eastern valley's service to London Paddington from all stations to Newport. The cost of a return ticket from Pontypool in 1960 was just under £2!

189. Crane Street station, which was the first of the Pontypool stations to be opened after completion of the line from Newport. Built by The Monmouthshire Railway and Canal Company, Crane Street opened in 1852. The station seen here is the newer enlarged premises which were constructed in 1858. Passenger services on this line were withdrawn on 30th April 1962, although the goods yard, seen on the left, remained in use until 31st October 1966. This photograph from about 1907 shows a train heading in the direction of Newport.

190. By the late 1950s, traditional steam-powered locomotives had given way to diesel multiple units on the valley's lines. This was much to the regret of many, despite the efficiencies of comfort and time-saving offered. The photograph on the left was taken from the driver's compartment of a diesel unit as it approached Pontnewynydd station in April 1962. The view looks in the direction of Abersychan and the platform is deserted except for a solitary railway employee.

191. Clarence Street Station, which was built by Mr Charles Liddell for the Newport, Abergavenny and Hereford Railway. This was situated on what was known as the Taff Vale extension line, built westward from Pontypool to link up with the Taff Vale Railway and opened as far as Crumlin Junction in 1855. The opening of Crumlin Viaduct in 1857 allowed further extension of the line to Pontllanfraith and ultimately to Neath and beyond. The line closed in 1964 and any remaining evidence of Clarence Street Station is hard to find.

192. This is the original Pontypool Road Station which was opened in 1854. Initially the station was called Newport Road and a Mr Henry Griffiths was appointed as the first station master. These early buildings and platforms were positioned on the south side of the road bridge but, by 1906 were unable to cope with the ever increasing volumes of traffic. Thus it was decided to construct a much larger station on the north side of the bridge as seen on the following photograph.

193. The new and extensive Pontypool Road Station which was completed and officially opened on 1st March 1909. This was a major freight and passenger station, with a platform length of almost a quarter of a mile; the second longest in Britain, surpassed only by Manchester's Victoria. The station today is but a shadow of its former self and has been renamed Pontypool and New Inn.

194. The magnitude of Pontypool Road is well evidenced by the presence of 34 members of staff pictured at the station in 1915. The facilities offered here in days gone by, even included the pleasantries of licensed refreshment rooms. Then came the unabated decline of rail travel during the 1960s, and Pontypool Road was all but demolished by local contractors W.J. Harris and Sons in 1970. The station is now un-manned and sees limited traffic between South Wales and the Midlands.

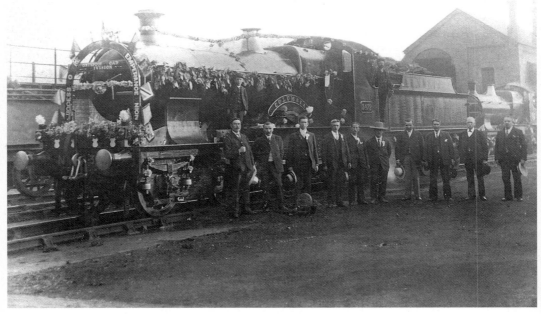

195. The busy engine sheds at Pontypool Road in about 1908, with a well-decorated locomotive No. 3472 'Columbia' 4-4-0 Bulldog class to be seen. A display on the front states 'Success to the GWR Temperance Union Pontypool Road Division', suggesting this to be a period of anti-alcohol feeling and religious revival in the district.

196. Little Mill Junction which was just a mile or two from Pontypool. This was opened by the Coleford, Monmouth, Usk and Pontypool Railway in 1856 and yet closed only a few years later in 1861. With the development of the G.W.R. however, the junction was reopened in 1883. On the left is the main line to Abergavenny, with a train heading in the direction of Pontypool. To the right is the branch line for services to Usk and Monmouth; note also a stationary wagon belonging to the former Little Mill Brick Company.

197. A group of railway workers take a break, although it is not absolutely certain where, in the Pontypool district the picture was taken. It is possibly at Little Mill marshalling yards or Pontnewynydd (Branches Fork), in the 1920s or '30s. The one gentleman positively identified is Mr. Arthur Griffiths, standing third from the right.

198/199. Two photographs of the former station, Panteg and Griffithstown. Built in 1879, it was originally called Panteg, the addition of Griffithstown coming some time later. The platforms were staggered and the photograph above shows the 'up' platform with the main station building and booking office. In days of steam, the locomotives would fill up here with water, in readiness for the up-valley journey to Blaenavon. The lower photograph shows the 'down' platform with Panteg Works in the background. Both of these photographs date from about 1907.

200. The busy and extensive junction of Coed-y-Gric, an area that has now been transformed by new roads and factory sites. On the left is the line for Pontypool and Blaenavon, and on the right, lines head for Pontypool Road and beyond. As can be seen on this 1915 photograph, this was a bustling and important part of the system. The engine in the foreground is a 2-6-2 T Type, No.3125 which was built in 1905.

201. Blaendare Road Halt with its quaint 'Pagoda-Style' waiting rooms. This Halt was opened by popular demand from the local residents, by The Great Western Railway on April 30th 1928. This was a period during which a number of these small Halts were being added to the branch lines of the G.W.R. Once a popular stop for pupils of nearby West Mon School, the exit on the left led passengers onto Victoria Road.

202. This concluding photograph concerning Pontypool's railway era is quite unique. It has been reproduced from a nineteenth century glass lantern slide and shows the original Pontypool Road Station as mentioned earlier in this chapter. A pre-1900 scene and amongst the interesting features is the porter's hat which bears the name Clarence Hotel; he probably having been sent to the station to collect some passengers, intent on staying at Pontypool's leading hotel.

Then and Now

This final chapter is devoted to a small, but important selection of photographs which will serve to remind today's observers of the sweeping changes that have affected the appearance of the Pontypool district so much in recent years.

203/204. Looking down Crane Street in 1905 and 1998 from a position outside The Globe Hotel. A very much-changed scene is before us, with virtually all of the left-hand side of the street now demolished except for a few remaining shops at the lower end.

205/206. Two photographs of George Street which were taken some fifty years apart. Above, on the left, was the bank (as seen on page 98) which adjoined a few shops and The Full Moon public house. This side of the street was demolished during the 1963 road-widening scheme. The 1998 view below, taken from the same spot, makes an interesting comparison.

207/208. Osborne Road is pictured above in 1908 thronging with pedestrians. The prominent building on the right is The Theatre Royal, formerly the Hanbury Assembly Rooms and later of course, The Royal Cinema. The shop facing the camera, at the end of the road, was later to become Williams and Jones, the gents' outfitters; their premises being one of the last to be demolished during the reconstruction of George Street. The building on the immediate left with the balcony is the local Conservative Club. The picture below shows how it all looked in the Spring of 1998.

209/210. The Town Bridge, which has seen some major changes over the years. The upper photograph is prior to the construction of the new bridge in 1924 and two surveyors, Bryn Jones and Arthur Williams are seen at work. On the left is a former building belonging to Sandbrook and Dawe and in the centre, a silent film starring Harold Lloyd is advertised at West's Pavilion Pontnewynydd. In comparison with today's picture, it will be noted that the cottages behind the advertisement hoarding now form the site of the Salvation Army Citadel, the building having been opened in 1937.

211/212. Anyone who may have left the Pontypool district at some time and not returned in recent years, will perhaps find the changes here, at Pontymoile corner, hard to comprehend. The picture above is from the 1930s, with all of the buildings in view now gone. On the left are Panteg Council Offices and HFB Bakery. On the right is the former Pontymoile Mission, the last building to be pulled down to make way for the new road system now in place. Stood beside the handsome lamp is Mr Tom Tew. The lower photograph is taken from the same position more than sixty years later.

213/214. Above, it is October 1957 at Clarence Street Station and locomotive No.4229 with brake van, makes its way towards Hafodyrynys. Today's picture would almost be beyond recognition, were it not for a glimpse of Park View and a corner house on St. Matthews Road in the background.

215/216. No more than thirty years separate these two photographs taken at Pontnewynydd, and yet, as locals will know, much has changed. The Pavilion Cinema and Western Welsh garage are but a few places to reminisce about at this spot.

217/218. The main road leading through New Inn and, ninety years later a few alterations have taken place. Looking carefully at the upper photograph, a gateway can be seen in the hedge on the left. This marks the spot where the junction road leads to Griffithstown and the building just behind the trees is now the Greenlawn Social Club.

219/220. Picton Street, or to use its nineteenth-century name, Pickering Road. In the early 1900s, the street-lighting system appears to consist of just one gas lamp, and by its side is an unusual-looking water hydrant. The corner building directly opposite, was once the premises of Mr John Boyt, a local painter and decorator. Below in 1998 the scene is an all too familiar sight, one of traffic congestion.

Acknowledgements

I wish to offer sincere thanks to a number of friends and colleagues, without whose much valued help, this book might not have been possible and, to anyone I may have inadvertently omitted, please accept my humble apologies.

For the loan of some photographs and accompanying information, I am grateful to Mrs. B. Bannon, Mr. and Mrs. T. Cole, Mr. Ron Couzens, Mrs. Sybil Foster, Mr. and Mrs. R. Gwillim, Mr. Peter Jones, Mr. Graham Sherwood, Mrs. M. Sweeting and Mr. A. White.

I am particularly grateful to, and appreciative of the help, advice and encouragement given by two fellow local authors and very good friends, Louis Bannon and Malcolm Thomas. Thank you both very much indeed for your experience and esteemed guidance.

Finally, I am indebted to my wife Margaret, who has shown so much tolerance and understanding and, also provided valuable opinions without complaint over a long period of time.

Below is a selection of further titles available. Please send stamp to the Publishers for a detailed catalogue.

Blackwood Yesterday in Photographs - Book 1
by Ewart Smith   ISBN 0 9512181 6 6

Blackwood Yesterday in Photographs - Book 2
by Ewart Smith   ISBN 1 874538 65 4

Blackwood Yesterday in Photographs - Book 3
by Ewart Smith   ISBN 1 874538 76 X

Blaenavon Through the Years in Photographs - Volume 1
by Malcolm Thomas and John Lewis   ISBN 0 9512181 0 7

Blaenavon Through the Years in Photographs - Volume 2
by Malcolm Thomas and John Lewis   ISBN 0 9512181 3 1

Blaenavon Through the Years in Photographs - Volume 3
by Malcolm Thomas and John Lewis   ISBN 1 874538 10 7

Brynmawr, Beaufort and Blaina in Photographs - Volume 1
by Malcolm Thomas   ISBN 1 874538 15 8

Brynmawr, Beaufort and Blaina in Photographs - Volume 2
by Malcolm Thomas   ISBN 1 874538 26 3

Trinant in Photographs - Volume 1
by Clive Daniels   ISBN 1 874538 80 8

Collieries of the Sirhowy Valley
by Rayner Rosser   ISBN 1 874538 01 8

The Aneurin Bevan Inheritance
by Gareth Jones   ISBN 1 874538 17 4

Bargoed & Gilfach in Photographs - Volume 1
by Paul James   ISBN 1 874538 31 X

History of Webbs Brewery - Aberbeeg
by Ray Morris   ISBN 1 874538 46 8

A Look at Old Tredegar in Photographs - Volume 1
by Philip Prosser   ISBN 0 9512181 4 X

A Look at Old Tredegar in Photographs - Volume 2
by Philip Prosser   ISBN 1 874538 81 6

Caerleon 'Scenes Past' - Volume 1
by Norman Stevens   ISBN 1 874538 71 9

A Picture Book of Cwm - Volume 1
by Margaret Blackwell   ISBN 1 874538 66 2

The Place Names of Eastern Gwent
by Graham Osborne & Graham Hobbs   ISBN 1 874538 91 3

Remember Abergavenny - Volume 1
by Louis Bannon   ISBN 1 874538 75 1

Talgarth - Jewel of the Black Mountains - Volume 1
by Roger G. Williams   ISBN 1 874538 60 3

Talgarth - Jewel of the Black Mountains - Volume 2
by Roger G. Williams   ISBN 1 874538 36 0